Building a
Green Community

Ellen Rodger

Crabtree Publishing Company
www.crabtreebooks.com

Crabtree Publishing Company

www.crabtreebooks.com

Author: Ellen Rodger
Coordinating editor: Chester Fisher
Project Manager: Kavita Lad (Q2AMEDIA)
Art direction: Rahul Dhiman (Q2AMEDIA)
Design: Ranjan Singh (Q2AMEDIA)
Photo research: Akansha Srivastava (Q2AMEDIA)
Editor: Molly Aloian
Copy editor: Mike Hodge
Project editor: Robert Walker
Production coordinator: Katherine Kantor
Prepress technician: Katherine Kantor

Photographs: P3: Corbis (bottom left), Istockphoto (bottom right); P4: Roza / Dreamstime; P5: Istockphoto; P6: Alexey Samarin / Shutterstock; P7: iofoto / Shutterstock; P8: Alfred Eisenstaedt / Stringer / Time & Life Pictures / Getty Images; P9: Associated Press; P10: Jonathan Maddock / Istockphoto; P11: Boeing; P12: Stephen Ferry / Contributor / Getty Images; P13: SAYYID AZIM / ASSOCIATED PRESS; P14: Johnson Space Center / NASA; P15: Ronald C. Modra / Sports Imagery / Contributor / Getty Images; P16: Maxim Marmur / Associated Press; P17: Ted Soqui / Corbis; P18: David R. Frazier Photolibrary, Inc. / Alamy; P19: Kevin Morris / Getty images; P20: AGStockUSA, Inc. / Alamy; P21: J-C&D. Pratt / Photolibrary; P22: Jane Legate / Photolibrary; P23: Alex Pitt / Istockphoto; P23: Hadler / Stuhr / Getty Images; P24: JTB Photo / Photolibrary; P25: Denew / Alamy; P26: Ieva Geneviciene / Shutterstock; P27: Corbis; P28: Bryan Hemphill / Photolibrary; P29: Comstock (top), Shutterstock (bottom); P30: Mohammed Uraibi / Associated Press (top); P30: Mohammed Uraibi / Associated Press (middle); P30: Jeff Greenberg / Alamy.

Cover: Ashley Cooper / Alamy
Bedzed, the United Kingdom's largest eco village, located in Beddington, London.

Title page: Steve Geer / Istockphoto
Towering skyscrapers and bright summer flowers of downtown Chicago, Illinois.

Library and Archives Canada Cataloguing in Publication

Rodger, Ellen
    Building a green community / Ellen Rodger.

(Energy revolution)
Includes index.
ISBN 978-0-7787-2916-7 (bound).
--ISBN 978-0-7787-2930-3 (pbk.)

    1. Sustainable living--Juvenile literature. 2. Environmental protection--Citizen participation--Juvenile literature. I. Title. II. Series.

GE195.5.R63 2008   j333.72   C2008-901523-1

Library of Congress Cataloging-in-Publication Data

Rodger, Ellen.
    Building a green community / Ellen Rodger.
        p. cm. -- (Energy revolution)
    Includes index.
    ISBN-13: 978-0-7787-2930-3 (pbk. : alk. paper)
    ISBN-10: 0-7787-2930-3 (pbk. : alk. paper)
    ISBN-13: 978-0-7787-2916-7 (reinforced library binding : alk. paper)
    ISBN-10: 0-7787-2916-8 (reinforced library binding : alk. paper)
    1. Sustainable living--Juvenile literature. 2. Environmental protection--Citizen participation--Juvenile literature. 3. Environmental responsibility--Juvenile literature. 4. Green movement--Juvenile literature. I. Title. II. Series.

    TD171.7.R63 2008
    333.72--dc22   2008012076

Crabtree Publishing Company

www.crabtreebooks.com   1-800-387-7650

Published in Canada
Crabtree Publishing
616 Welland Ave.
St. Catharines, ON
L2M 5V6

Published in the United States
Crabtree Publishing
PMB16A
350 Fifth Ave., Suite 3308
New York, NY 10118

Published in the United Kingdom
Crabtree Publishing
White Cross Mills
High Town, Lancaster
LA1 4XS

Published in Australia
Crabtree Publishing
386 Mt. Alexander Rd.
Ascot Vale (Melbourne)
VIC 3032

Contents

Energy Conservation: "We Can Do It!"

"We Can Do It" was a slogan that appeared on posters made during **World War II**. One poster featured 'Rosie the Riveter,' a woman dressed in blue coveralls (shown below). The poster was originally intended to encourage women to enter the workforce in industry to replace the men who left to serve in the war. Today, the image of Rosie the Riveter represents a time when people came together as a society to reach a common goal. Today's energy challenge can be combatted in a similar way. Together, we can work to save our planet from the pollution caused by burning fossil fuels by learning to conserve energy and developing alternative energy sources.

We Can Do It!

WAR PRODUCTION CO-ORDINATING COMMITTEE

Being Green

Green living is a term used to describe a way of life that includes caring for the **environment**, or all the plants, animals, humans, and other living and non-living things on Earth. For years, scientists have been gathering evidence that proves the way many humans live today is harming the environment. Humans use and abuse the environment through their **consumption habits**. The cars people drive spew exhaust that pollutes the air. The food many people eat is treated with harmful chemicals that poison soil and water. Humans buy too much and do not recycle enough.

Changing the Way We Live

To preserve the environment, everyone on the planet has to start living differently. Green living means changing the way people drive, eat, buy, grow things, and shop. Each change that humans make to their lifestyles has an impact, or an effect, on Earth. Some people believe green living means trying to make as little impact on Earth as possible in order not to damage it. To do this, people should try to ensure that everything they make, buy, or use can be recycled, remade, or buried in the ground where it can **decompose**, or rot, and give life to the soil.

Automobile-exhaust emissions add carbon dioxide and other gases to the atmosphere. The emissions are a major source of excess greenhouse gases that contribute to global warming.

What is Sustainability?

When people talk about the environment, they often use the term 'sustainability' as an example of something good. Sustainability means keeping something at a certain level to maintain health and survival. Sustaining the environment means repairing the damage done and preventing more damage from occurring in the future. Environmental sustainability requires more than caring for the environment. It requires a level of care for the way other people live, as well as their **economic** and social well-being. Environmentalists help care for the environment. Caring about the environment means caring about what you throw in the trash, how crops are grown, and what fuels are used to power automobiles. It also means caring about how people in other countries live and breathe.

Growing your own pesticide-free vegetables and fruits in a garden helps the environment.

Warming planet

Earth's climate has been gradually warming over the last 40 years, and most scientists believe humans are to blame. Humans burn fossil fuels such as oil, natural gas, and coal to power cars, produce electricity, and heat and cool homes. Burning fossil fuels creates greenhouse gases such as carbon dioxide that trap the sun's heat in Earth's atmosphere. The trapped heat raises Earth's temperature in a process called global warming. Global warming is changing the world's weather patterns and making the planet warmer. The only way to stop global warming is to change and reduce our dependency on fossil fuels.

Energy Consumers

Everyone on Earth is an energy consumer. They use the planet's natural fuels, such as oil, gas, coal, or wood, to cook food or power vehicles. These fuels pollute the environment. Humans consume some forms of energy that harm the environment more than other forms.

Fossil Fuels

Fossil fuels are the most common sources of energy used throughout the world today. They are a part of our daily lives. Crude oil, or petroleum, is used to make gasoline that fuels automobiles and planes. It is also processed and used in the **petrochemical industry** to make everyday items such as aspirin, some household cleaners, and plastics. Coal is used to produce electric power for heating and lighting.

It is also used in industry to make tar, steel, **fertilizers**, and even medicines. Natural gas is used to heat homes and offices. It also provides the raw material for making paints, plastics, antifreeze, explosives, and propane for outdoor barbeque grills.

Millions of Years

Fossil fuels were formed millions of years ago from dead and decaying plants and animals. Most fossil fuels lie buried deep within the ground. They must be mined or drilled. They must also be **refined** before they can be used. The problem with fossil fuels is that using them creates excess carbon-dioxide, or CO_2, emissions. Carbon dioxide is one of the greenhouse gases scientists believe is responsible for global warming.

Petrochemical plants emit harmful carbon dioxide, a greenhouse gas that contributes to global warming.

Alternative Energies

All over the world, the demand for energy and the use of fossil fuels is increasing. People want to continue driving and flying. They want appliances that use a lot of energy, such as refrigerators and air conditioners. To cut down on the use of fossil fuels, some people have turned to alternative energy sources. Alternative energy sources do not pollute the environment or release greenhouse gases. These sources include solar energy, which uses the power of the sun's rays, and wind power, which converts the movement of the wind into energy. Other alternative energy sources use the heat underneath Earth's crust or the power of ocean tides to create energy for everyday use.

Nuclear Option

Some people believe nuclear energy can provide power without harming the environment. Nuclear energy produces electricity through a process called fission. Fission splits uranium atoms into parts, releasing energy. Uranium is an element in a metal ore that is mined. Nuclear power plants create a lot of energy without producing greenhouse gases, but they still produce waste. Nuclear waste is radioactive, and in high levels, it can kill people, animals, and plants. There are 450 nuclear power plants around the world. The plants dispose of radioactive waste by diluting it so it is less radioactive and isolating it or burying it deep under ground. Researchers are working on ways to produce cleaner nuclear power and create less radioactive waste.

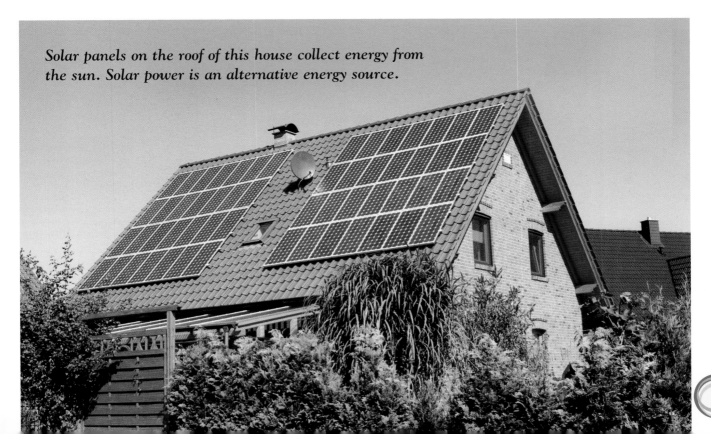

Solar panels on the roof of this house collect energy from the sun. Solar power is an alternative energy source.

A Wake-Up Call

Fifty years ago, most people did not think that the way they lived their lives had any impact on the environment. After World War II, the North American economy was booming. More people than ever before had the money to buy cars and appliances. New housing developments with large lawns and garages sprawled out from cities. By using chemical fertilizers and pesticides, farms began producing greater **yields** of crops. Factories were making new plastic products using petrochemicals. No one thought this growth had an environmental cost.

Silent Spring

In the late 1950s, American **ecologist** Rachel Carson noticed that birds were dying at an alarming rate near areas that had been sprayed with a chemical pesticide called DDT. Carson wrote a book called *Silent Spring*, which explained that DDT, the most powerful pesticide ever created, was killing birds by poisoning their food sources. It also poisoned the land and water and worked its way up the **food chain** to cause disease in humans. Carson believed humans were a part of nature and could not abuse the environment without suffering the cost.

Like all ecologists, Rachel Carson believed that all living things were connected, or a part of the cycle of life.

Environmental Protection

Silent Spring caused a stir in the scientific community and is credited with starting the modern environmental movement. In 1970, the book influenced the U.S. government, which created the Environmental Protection Agency (EPA). This government agency helps protect the environment and prevent pollution. Despite chemical-company protests, the EPA banned DDT in the United States in 1972. Many other countries followed with similar bans, and more people began to think about how to protect the environment.

Greenpeace and Activism

Since 1971, the environmental group Greenpeace has been fighting against the destruction of forests, global warming, overfishing, and other environmental issues. Greenpeace began as an activist group in Vancouver, Canada, when a group of people banded together to protest nuclear testing in Alaska. The activists felt that the U.S. government was putting its own people and world peace at risk by testing nuclear weapons underneath Alaska's Aleutian Islands. Greenpeace hired a boat and sailed to the testing site, trying to disrupt or end the testing. Despite Greenpeace protests, the test went ahead as scheduled.

The action helped form one of the world's most well-known environmental groups. Today, Greenpeace is an international organization that depends on donations to continue public environmental education and to launch activist campaigns. Greenpeace believes that protecting and conserving the environment means changing people's attitudes toward the environment. Activists use nonviolent means to push individual people, companies, and governments into changing their behavior.

Greenpeace activism includes taking companies and countries to court to stop harmful or illegal activities that harm the environment.

Ecological Footprint

Since 1970, the world has lost 30 percent of its spaces and resources through forest destruction and the overuse of water and soil. During that same time, most of the world's growth has occurred in urban areas or cities. As the world's population grows, the need for more resources grows, as well. Humans are not doing a good job of conserving what already exists.

Urban Areas

Half of the world's population lives in urban areas. All those people living in cities require clean water, public transportation, and power. They also need food, the resources to cook it, and waste-disposal systems to get rid of their sewage and trash. The energy, products, food, and water—the resources they use—must come from somewhere.

Ecological Footprint

In 1992, scientists Mathis Wackernagel and William Rees developed the Ecological Footprint. The Ecological Footprint is a method for calculating how much land or water a group of humans needs to produce the all the resources it consumes. Everyone uses resources, but some people use more than others.

A footprint is a mark that you leave behind. You can calculate your Ecological Footprint or your family's footprint at www.ecofoot.org or www.kidsfootprint.org

Raising Awareness

Using Wackernagel and Rees' method helps make people aware of their impact on the planet. Wackernagel and Rees' goal is to create a sustainable environment. A sustainable environment is one where what is taken from the environment equals or is less than what is put into the environment. Wackernagel and Rees have developed separate Ecological Footprints for the world, for individual countries, and for activities. For example, they can figure out how much carbon dioxide is created from burning fossil fuels from flying in a jet. Their Ecological Footprints determine Earth's **biocapacity**, or its ability to handle wastes made by humans.

Wasting the World

North Americans are the world's greatest resource wasters. They buy too much, use too many fossil fuels, and throw away too much. According to Wackernagel and Rees, if they continue to use Earth's resources at the current rate, North Americans will need eight Earths to supply all their needs.

Your Footprint

The Ecological Footprint idea can apply to everyone. A Footprint is a measure of your impact on Earth, including how you live, eat, travel, and how much energy you use. Your Footprint will be large if you are driven to school in a car, eat packaged and processed foods, do not recycle, and fly a lot. Those activities use a lot of energy and waste resources. If you walked or biked to school, you would not burn any fossil fuels. Public transportation and school buses move a lot of people to the same place, thereby using less fossil fuel than ten cars moving twenty people do. A lot of energy is used to make and transport packaged and processed foods to grocery-store shelves. Recycling takes a product and remakes it into something else, saving it from the garbage dump.

Airplanes emit an incredible amount of carbon dioxide into the atmosphere, adding to the greenhouse effect.

Conservation Tip

Anybody can be an activist. All it takes is a cause and some commitment. Many environmental groups welcome new members. Most need volunteers or the money that supporters donate. You can also form your own environmental or green group to promote and protect the environment. Many groups start small with only a few members and one cause. After some time, the group grows and adds other causes.

Land Conservation

Every day, thousands of trees are cut down to make wood and paper products and to clear land for farming. Newly planted trees replace only a small percentage of these trees. The world's forests are important to life on Earth. They provide a habitat for wild animals. Trees also remove the carbon dioxide from the atmosphere and replace it with oxygen.

People and Forests

The growth of cities and **urban sprawl** has damaged many forests. Trees are cut to build new houses. Some cities have green belts of trees that improve the air quality, but many cities have no forests at all. In some areas of the world, forests cleared for farming cannot support crops because without the trees, the soil is not **fertile**. Without tree roots to keep the dirt in place, soil is scattered by wind and rain.

Green Forests

Sustainable forestry is a green-living practice that involves planting trees and conserving forests. Trees are used as lumber for construction and to make paper products. Sustainable forestry includes selective cutting, or not cutting all of the trees in a forest, and not cutting **old-growth forests**. Old-growth forests contain trees that are hundreds and sometimes thousands of years old. Many environmentalists believe old-growth forests should not be cut down because they help us learn about forests.

Cattle ranching is a major cause for the decrease in the amount of forestland in Brazil's Amazon rain forest. The cattle are raised for export to Europe and North America. Over the last 30 years, an area the size of Alabama has been cleared of all trees.

Conservation Tip

You can protect forests by watching, limiting, and changing your consumption habits. Try to use less paper or use both sides of a sheet of paper. Recycle the paper you do use, and buy recycled paper products.

Maathai's Green Belt

Wangari Maathai is known as the "tree woman" of Africa. Maathai is an environmentalist and political activist from Kenya. She founded the Green Belt Movement to push environmental issues in that country and other parts of Africa. Members of the Green Belt Movement have planted over 30 million trees across Kenya. They have also protested plans to build buildings and parking lots on forested land. Wood is a popular fuel for cooking in many parts of Africa, and many forests have been cut down for fuel. Planting trees helps restore forests and prevent soil erosion. The Movement not only plants trees, but funds tree nurseries and trains women to protect their local environments. For her activism, Maathai has been thrown in jail, and she and her supporters have been beaten. Despite imprisonment, beatings, and threats, Maathai continues her activism. She helped protect the Karura Forest near Nairobi from being sold off in parts. Maathai has written several books about her activism and believes that environmental issues are human-rights issues. She won the Nobel Peace Prize in 2004 for her contribution to sustainable development, democracy, and peace.

Wangari Maathai (holding tree) plants a tree with Barack Obama.

Water Conservation

When astronauts first sent back images of Earth taken from space, people were astounded at how blue the planet looked. In fact, they began to call it "the big blue ball." Earth looks blue from space because water from rivers, lakes, and oceans covers more than 70 percent of the planet. Water is one of the world's most important natural resources, and only one to three percent is drinkable. That scarcity should make humans more careful about how they treat rivers, lakes, and oceans. Unfortunately, pollution is a major threat to fresh-water supplies, and many of the world's oceans have been overfished. Global warming is also affecting the world's oceans and water supplies by melting glaciers and polar ice caps.

From outer space, Earth looks like a big blue ball.

Water Pollution

People once thought that lakes and oceans were so large that small amounts of harmful chemicals and sewage would disperse, or disappear in the water. They believed this pollution would not harm the water or the fish and plants living in it. This is not true. Chemical runoff from factories has polluted many streams, rivers, and lakes. **Sewage-treatment plants** are often located near bodies of water. Untreated waste from water-treatment plants sometimes leaks out during storms. It enters lakes, rivers, and streams, causing bacteria to grow and disturbing the water's natural balance.

Conservation Tip

North Americans use more water for household activities than any other population on Earth. Water is wasted on baths, long showers, watering lawns and golf courses, and washing cars! If all households used water-saving technology, such as low-flush toilets, it would save an estimated 60 billion to 80 billion gallons (224 billion to 303 billion liters) of water per day! For more tips on using water wisely, go to www.wateruseitwisely.com.

Laws and Regulations

Most countries and cities have water-quality laws and regulations that are supposed to ensure rivers, lakes, and oceans are not polluted. People and businesses do not always follow these rules, and the government does not always enforce them. Individuals can help protect water supplies by monitoring their own use of water. They can also make sure that the products they use in their own homes are not harmful to the environment. They can make small changes such as not buying or eating fish that are overfished. They can also use household soaps and detergents that do not contain phosphates. Phosphates are chemicals that are found in high levels in some cleaning products, fertilizers, and pesticides. When they are flushed into sewage systems, they make **algae** grow in water. Too much algae reduces the oxygen supply in the water, killing fish.

Swordfish are large, fast ocean fish, which were in danger from overfishing. In 1998, an environmental group, the National Resources Defence Council, launched a campaign to convince chefs not to serve swordfish in restaurants. The campaign was successful, and the U.S. government also banned the sale and import of the fish. Swordfish stocks are now recovering in some parts of the world.

15

Air Conservation

The air we breathe is vital to our survival. Many television weather stations give daily air-quality reports to their viewers. For urban areas, these reports include smog conditions and warnings to people with lung diseases. Sometimes the smog is so bad that it can kill.

The quality of the air we breathe is getting worse every day because of the many harmful gases that are pumped into the atmosphere.

Air Pollution

Air pollution occurs when gases, fumes, and chemicals collect in the air in amounts that are harmful to humans and other living things. These gases and chemicals are a result of how we live today. Burning fossil fuels for heat and to power automobiles puts more carbon dioxide, nitrogen dioxide, and sulphur dioxide into Earth's atmosphere. These gases, in turn, contribute to global warming.

Chemicals In the Air

Chemical emissions from manufacturing plants and electric plants that burn coal for energy create acid rain. Acid rain erodes buildings and kills life in lakes and rivers. Chemicals in our air, such as nitrogen dioxide, inflame the lungs and make it hard to breathe. Nitric oxide, the chemical that causes hazy days, harms plants and can even corrode metals or cause them to fall apart.

How to Stop It

Earth's atmosphere contains many chemicals and gases, including nitrogen and oxygen. Most of these chemicals and gases also occur naturally. Burning fossil fuels adds even more. Earth's atmosphere cannot cope with the additional gases. The increased use of chemicals used by humans in their daily life is destroying nature's balance. The only way to reverse the damage and improve air quality is to change the way we live.

Fixing the Ozone Hole

Earth's atmosphere is divided into layers. Ozone is a layer of gas in the Earth's stratosphere level of the atmosphere. Ozone absorbs harmful ultraviolet radiation (UV) from the sun. During the 1950s, scientists began to measure the ozone. By the 1970s, they had determined that there was a hole in the ozone over the continent of Antarctica. The hole allowed UV radiation to seep in. UV radiation causes eye damage and cancer and contributes to a harmful chemical smog. Human use of chlorofluorocarbons (CFCs) caused the hole.

CFCs are gases and liquids that are used in refrigerators, car air conditioners, aerosol spray cans, and even hamburger wrappers. After several protests by environmental groups in 1987, many countries agreed to reduce their use of CFCs and to phase out use altogether over time. The 24-country agreement, called the Montreal Protocol after the city where it was signed, limited CFC production. Many CFCs have been banned, but scientists report that the ozone is still under threat. It may take another 50 years for it to recover.

Old-style aerosol spray cans were banned after the Montreal Protocol. It was one of the first worldwide agreements on environmental issues.

Green In the City

Most of the world's population lives in cities and urban metropolitan areas. Enormous city populations require a lot of land for housing, industry, and roads. As cities grow, they sprawl out beyond their original boundaries to absorb smaller villages, suburbs, and, often, good farmland. Urban sprawl causes environmental problems, including pollution from garbage, destruction of forests and wetlands, and a need for better water and sewage treatment. Each new building requires land, water services, and trash collection. Cities cannot grow indefinitely. City planners, or the people who determine how a city should grow, are studying plans for new and sustainable growth that will not harm the environment.

Greening the City

Green cities are livable cities that provide good mass transportation, such as buses and subways, and air that is clean. The city of Chattanooga, Tennessee, was once very polluted. It worked hard to clean up its act. During the 1970s, the city had crumbling buildings and the most polluted air of any city in the United States. Drivers had to turn their car lights on during the day because there was so much pollution from soot that they could not see clearly. During the 1980s, Chattanooga passed new air-quality laws that limited industrial air and water pollution. The cleanup required businesses, government, and ordinary citizens to work together. Chattanooga developed a hybrid electric-powered bus service, and a company there now makes city buses. Over one million people a year take the bus instead of using cars, improving the air quality. Chattanooga now sells buses to other cities.

Some cities encourage upward development, or constructing high-density city buildings that are many floors tall. These replace hundreds of smaller houses.

BedZED: Building wisely

As cities run out of space, city planners are using brownfields for new housing. Brownfields are existing city lands that may have been polluted by industry in the past. They must be cleaned up before they can be used again. Brownfield restoration and building is an excellent example of sustainable development. One successful brownfield restoration is the Beddington Zero Energy Development or BedZED project near London, England. A total of 82 houses, 17 apartments, and working spaces were built in 2002 on a former industrial site that had been cleaned up. BedZED is unusual because it uses zero energy, or only the energy from on-site renewable sources. The material used to build BedZED came from less than 35 miles (56 kilometers) away, which cut down on the pollution created to transport building material. All BedZED houses have solar panels, which reduce the use of electricity. The development uses tree waste, such as wood from branches and twigs, to fuel a heat and power plant. BedZED buildings are also well insulated, which prevents heat from being lost in winter and keeps them cooler in summer. At BedZED, rainwater is collected and reused, and waste is recycled. Residents use public transportation or carpool and drive special cars. These autos are powered by electricity or liquefied petroleum gas (LPG), a gas that does not use ozone-destroying CFCs. BedZed has been so successful that its residents use 57 percent less hot water and 25 percent less electricity than other United Kingdom residents.

The BedZED development grew out of a desire to build a community that produced as much energy from renewable sources as it used. This is the definition of a sustainable green community.

Conservation Tip

Trash collection is a service paid through tax dollars. If your city has a recycling program, make sure you learn how to use it. Tossing recyclable cans, paper, or bottles in the trash wastes valuable landfill or garbage dump space and tax dollars.

Green On the Farm

The way we grow food has changed dramatically over the past 50 years. The introduction of massive mechanical planters and harvesters, chemical fertilizers, and pesticides has allowed farmers to grow more crops on more land.

Sustainable Agriculture

Sustainable agriculture is a term that describes farming that is efficient, does not harm the environment, meets human needs for food, and provides an adequate salary for farmers and farm workers. Some countries have laws or policies that encourage sustainability.

Environmental Regulations

Farmers in North America and many other areas of the world have environmental regulations that they must follow. For example, they cannot allow animal manure near streams so the manure does not pollute drinking water. Sustainable agriculture is intended to limit the harmful effects of farming on the environment.

Terminator seeds are crop seeds that have been scientifically altered in a laboratory so that they repel pests. Seed companies control the use of terminator seeds. Many farmers do not like terminator seeds because they can only be used for one season. Farmers must continually buy more seed from seed companies every year.

What is Sustainability?

Farmers know that the way they treat their soil has a direct impact on the amount and quality of their crops. In sustainable agriculture, farmers rotate their crops, or regularly plant different crops on their land. One year, they may grow corn, and another year, they will grow soybeans on the same land. Corn, cotton, and tobacco deplete the soil of nutrients. Soybeans and other legumes add nitrogen, which is essential for good soil. To reduce soil erosion, or the loss of good topsoil, farmers do not till the soil, or plow and churn it. Instead, seeds are planted along with the remains of the previous season's crop. No-till farming wastes less energy.

Animals and Pests

Many commercial farmers use chemical pesticides and **herbicides** on crops. Chemical pesticides and herbicides help produce high yields of blemish- and disease-free crops. Many people worry about their long-term risks. These chemicals can kill more than their intended targets of insects. They are also expensive for farmers. Some farmers are turning to old-fashioned or alternative methods to rid their crops of pests and diseases. They are keeping **free-range** chickens, ducks, and geese that eat insects or raising goats and sheep that eat weeds.

Organic Farming

Organic farming does not use chemical pesticides and fertilizers, drugs and growth hormones for animals, or genetically modified seeds. Organic farming is much like how farming used to be over 100 years ago. Organic farms are smaller than nonorganic farms, and they produce fewer crops and animals. They also require more labor. Farmers pull weeds instead of using chemical herbicides. They also plant crops that help other plants stay free of disease. They must use natural, or organic, pesticides and fertilizers instead of chemical ones. To be called organic, farms must follow a set of standards. In some areas of the world, the standards say farms must be free of pesticide use for several years. Organic farmers are also very concerned about the health of their soil. They conserve the soil by practicing no-till farming. Organic farming is gaining popularity. People are buying more organic produce and meat because they believe it is healthier.

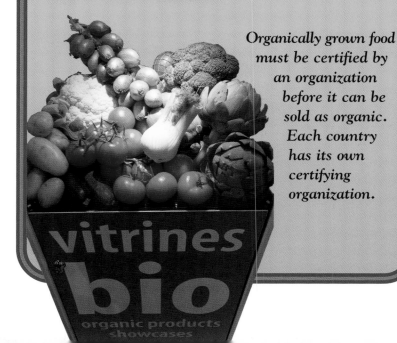

Organically grown food must be certified by an organization before it can be sold as organic. Each country has its own certifying organization.

The Green Home

About 80 percent of the energy used in the world today comes from **non-renewable** fossil fuels. Scientists estimate that supplies of some of those fossil fuels will run out within 50 years. It only makes sense to conserve what there is and find alternative energy sources for the future. Making your home a green home is one way to conserve energy. A green home is one where energy is not wasted.

(left) Manicured lawns are not natural. They require a lot of water to stay green and energy to cut and keep free of weeds. Use a push mower instead of an electric or gas-powered mower. You could also plant grasses and plants that are native to your area.

(below) Hang your clothes outside to dry to save electricity normally used in a dryer.

Green-Home Strategies

A green home is one that suits your needs and is not too big. A 7,000-square-foot (650-square-meter) home for two or three people will make a big footprint, even if the home is **ecologically efficient**.

1. Passive solar design is an energy-saving technology that captures the sun's energy and reduces the need for other forms of heating. Solar collectors can provide hot water for home use, and **photovoltaic panels** convert energy into electricity. Insulation helps keep the home warm in winter without turning the thermostat up and cool in summer.

2. Energy-efficient windows and doors keep cold air from entering the house in winter and hot air from entering in summer. Turn the thermostat down by three degrees to reduce fuel use.

3. Gray water is used household water such as bathwater, shower water, and water used for doing laundry. Some green homes have gray-water-collection systems that store the water so it can be used again to water lawns and trees. Gray-water collection cuts down on water consumption.

4. Off-the-grid homes do not rely on outside supplies of water, power, or natural gas for heating or cooking. Their energy does not come from a power plant. All of the daily supplies of electricity to power lights and machines come from on-site solar or wind power or solar panels and windmills. More people are choosing to live off the grid because it reduces their Ecological Footprint.

5. In the bathroom, showers use less water than baths do. A high-efficiency showerhead uses 60 percent less water than a regular showerhead does. A dual-flush toilet uses less water to flush the toilet. Most toilets use about 3 gallons (11 liters) of water in a single flush. Dual-flush toilets use less than half that to do the same job.

The Three Rs

Most people do not think about what they throw in the garbage can, where that trash goes, or what impact it has on the environment. On average, North Americans produce four pounds (1.8 kilograms) of garbage each day. In the United States alone, 210 million tons (190 million metric tons) of trash is created each year. Most of that garbage is sent to city dumps or landfills. A landfill is a piece of land where garbage is sorted, stored, or buried.

North Americans create more garbage than any other people on Earth. The amount of trash created has tripled since 1960, mostly because people buy more stuff.

Wasteful Society

In landfills, trash does not decompose quickly. It can take decades to disintegrate. Steel never decomposes. The purpose of a landfill is to hide trash from public view. When it is full, the land must be monitored for **toxins** for years. Since landfills fill up quickly and there is only so much land that is suitable for dumping, it makes sense to cut down on the amount of trash that is made. Cutting back requires a new way of thinking about what goes in the garbage. Many things are tossed in the trash without a second thought. Check your trash can. Is it filled with wrappers, cardboard, and plastic or paper cups? If so, you can do something about it.

Reducing What You Use

One way to become more green and reduce your impact on the environment is to reduce, reuse, and recycle. Reducing means cutting down on what you buy and use. For example, you can reduce your use of energy by wearing a warm wool sweater on cold days instead of asking your parents to turn the heat up. You can also walk more and use the car less. If you like prepackaged foods such as frozen pizzas, think about having them once every two weeks instead of once or twice a week. Prepackaged foods are wrapped in a lot of plastic and cardboard, and they usually travel long distances to the grocery store. Their manufacture and transportation uses more gasoline, which is created from fossil fuels. Burning fossil fuels contributes to global warming.

Reusing Items

Reusing clothing and household materials was once a way of life. Instead of buying disposable cleaning cloths, people cut up old sheets and used them to do housework. Today, many people prefer to buy new. What is wrong with reusing items and wearing hand-me-downs? They help the environment. Many studies say that up to 20 percent of what is thrown in the garbage can be reused. It is more green to have an item repaired instead of replacing it.

Instead of throwing out household items that they no longer use, people often sell them at street fairs or rummage sales. These items get a new life in someone else's home instead of ending up in a landfill.

Making New Paper

Ever wonder what happens to newspaper when it is recycled? After being picked up at the curb, paper is sent to a recycling center, where it is sorted and sent to factories that reuse the material. Paper is mixed with water to create a mushy pulp. The pulp passes through a screen that removes goop such as glue and staples. The pulp is then squeezed flat, rolled, and dried to create new paper.

Shop and Swop

Reusing includes finding new uses for materials. Glass food jars can hold anything from change to pencils or buttons. With your parents' permission, hold a clothing swap with your friends or give your old clothing to a charity. Try shopping at a used-clothing shop. They often stock fashionable clothing at a good price. Shopping there will make you feel better about your impact on the environment. Reuse paper and paper products. Use both sides of a paper for writing or drawing. Newspapers, especially the comics, can be used as gift wrap. After the gift is opened, the newspaper wrap can be recycled.

Recycling

Recycling is one of the easiest and most important green actions. If your city has a recycling program, learn how it works. Recycling programs require you to sort plastic, paper, and cans into different recycling boxes. In North America, one in every four plastic bottles is not recycled. Make sure that you do not throw a recyclable container in the trash. Check the container's label. Most have symbols on the back that tell you whether they can be recycled. Think before you throw anything out. Ask yourself: Can this be recycled? If your school does not have a recycling program, ask your teacher how you can help set one up.

Remember that recycling saves forests by reducing the number of trees needed to make paper. It also saves energy, landfill space, and water because many products made from recycled materials use less water in the manufacturing process.

Do not throw everything out with the garbage. Separate everything that can be recycled and put it in a separate, clearly marked box or bin.

Wartime Recycling Drives

Recycling is not new. During World War II, recycling was a necessity. Entire communities came together to gather material for the war effort. Factories in North America needed raw materials to build aircraft, tanks, and ships. During the war, raw materials such as rubber and metal were in short supply. At that time, rubber for automobile and aircraft tires came from rubber tree plants that grew only in tropical areas of the world. Enemy ships cut off ocean shipping routes and sank supply ships during the war. With no new supplies making their way to North America, people were forced to make due with what they had. People pitched in by collecting old rubber tires, used pots and pans, bottles, and even leftover bones. Bones were boiled to make glue for manufacturing aircraft and glycerin for making bombs. Rubber tires were recycled to make more tires. Pots, pans, and tin cans were melted down to make jeeps and armored vehicles. Everyone worked together to gather old household waste and bring it to recycling stations. Often, children pushed wagons from house to house, collecting for the war effort.

Recycling drives during World War II brought communities together to fight for a common cause. Old household pots and pans were melted into metal to make aircraft.

Green Shopping

How we shop and what we buy have enormous impacts on the environment. Shopping is one practice that we have control over. We can choose what products to buy and where we buy them.

Why Buy?

Sometimes people buy because they need things, and sometimes they buy because they want to display their wealth or position. Buying simply for the sake of buying or to show off is not green. Green shopping includes buying well-made merchandise that will last a long time and repairing things instead of always replacing them.

Shopping has become a hobby instead of a necessity. Be aware of how advertising makes you want to buy a product and resist the urge to buy just for the sake of buying.

Green Products

Today, many stores carry green products. Stores know that consumers, or buyers, want to purchase products that are better for the environment. A green product should be one that does not consume a lot of fossil-fuel energy to produce or run, can be recycled or is made of recycled materials, and is not shipped from thousands of miles away. Shipping products from far away consumes gasoline and adds greenhouse gases to the environment.

What to Buy

It is hard to know what products to buy and what purchases should be avoided. Here are a few tips for green shopping:

• Use reusable cloth bags for shopping. It cuts down on the need for plastic or paper bags.
• Buy fresh food instead of packaged and processed food. Fresh food tastes better and is better for you.
• Try to buy organic food, and buy from local sources such as farmers' markets as much as possible.
• Avoid heavily packaged products such as toys that are encased in hard plastic. Plastic is made from petrochemicals and it does not biodegrade easily in a landfill.
• Buy from retailers who care about the environment, their employees, and suppliers. If a store sells products produced with **sweatshop labor**, the store probably does not care about the environment. Green products should be produced using sustainable principles, including the principle of fair pay and treatment for the people who make the product.

The 100-Mile Diet

In 2005, Alisa Smith and James Mackinnon decided to reduce their carbon footprint, or the amount of greenhouse gases they contributed to the planet, by changing the way they ate. They read that the average North American eats foods that have traveled 1,500 miles (2,414 kilometers) from their source to the plate. Smith and Mackinnon decided to launch a year-long experiment where they would eat only foods that were grown or raised within 100 miles (160 kilometers) of their home in Vancouver, Canada. The pair learned that they could eat well without harming the environment. They shopped at small stores and local farmers' markets. They also learned how to garden and grow their own food, and can, or preserve, food when it was in season. Smith and Mackinnon ate a lot of potatoes at first and had to give up favorite foods such as chocolate. After all, cocoa beans do not grow anywhere near Vancouver! They discovered how food grows and when different foods are in season, something most people do not think about when shopping at a grocery store. Smith and Mackinnon wrote a book about their experience that has inspired other people to eat similar diets in their areas, and they still eat mostly local food.

Smith and Mackinnon ate a lot of apples on their diet, because apples grow within 100 miles (160 kilometers) of their home.

Chocolate and bananas were two foods that Smith and Mackinnon did not eat on their diet because both are tropical foods.

Conservation Tip

It takes energy to make, advertise, and transport products. Buy products that can be recycled or are made from recycled materials. Check the label to see where the product is made. Energy Star labels on appliances means they are more energy efficient.

Timeline

Food can be stored and transported from one place to another.

Buying fresh, locally-grown fruits at the market is more green than buying prepackaged foods.

Green living is not a new concept. Environmentalism is an idea that is thousands of years old. Many ancient civilizations understood that how they treated the land and water around them had a direct impact on their own well-being. If they farmed carelessly, removing nutrients from the soil, they had to move on and find another place to live. Modern quests to live more comfortably and acquire more things are harming the planet. This time, there is no place to move. Humans have to change the way they live to clean up the planet. Here is a list of some important milestones in the history of environmentalism.

535-500 B.C.

The Ancient Romans build sewers to carry waste and aqueducts to bring water to Roman cities. They store and conserve water during times of drought. The Roman Emperor Justinian declares, "by law of nature these things are common to mankind: the air, running water, the sea, and consequently the shores of the sea."

1300-1360 A.D.

The English burn "black rocks," or coal, for heating and cooking. King Edward I forbids the burning of coal in London when government is in session because it produces sooty pollution.

1388

English law prohibits throwing garbage into the streets, rivers, and waterways of cities.